P9-DFG-287

Decorating with Photographs

BY WAYNE FLOYD

AMPHOTO
American Photographic Book Publishing Co., Inc.
NEW YORK

Library of Congress Catalog Card No. 65-17121

Published in New York by Amphoto, and simultaneously in Toronto, Canada, by Ambassador Books, Ltd.

Contents

TO DOLORES
for her inspiration
and willing assistance

CHAPTER 1

Fitting Photographs Into Your Home Decor

Are you confused about how to display your pictures? Are you at a loss when it comes to deciding where to hang them?

This book will give you some pointers that will help you to show off your pictures to best advantage. No matter how much or how little you wish to use photographs as decoration in your home, you will find some valuable pointers in this book. You may be only a snapshooter, but proud of your handiwork, and you will learn of many simple ways to display your pictures, even the small ones.

If you go into photography on a larger scale, and make your own enlargements of portraits, scenics, close-ups, you will be interested in some of the ideas for incorporating pictures very extensively into your home decor. If, on the other hand, you are among the majority who are interested in pictures of your family and depend on the professional photographer to get the best possible results, you have even more reason to use care and planning in decorating with photographs. Whether the portrait photographer you choose is in a small town or a great city, he will be an expert at photographing the smallest to the biggest occasion of your life—a new baby, a wedding, a graduation or an anniversary. It is up to you to make maximum use of his professional eye by incorporating these pictures into your decorating scheme to their best advantage.

The main purpose of this book is to help you to get your pictures out of drawers and boxes so they can be seen and appreciated. How well you succeed, how simple or elaborate your ideas, depends on your own ingenuity and taste—and to a certain extent, your budget.

Portrait photographs, so popular in years past, are back in style—but in a new format. Even in small homes and apartments, photographs are being hung on the wall with the aplomb usually accorded oil paintings, and there are increasing numbers of family portraits on view where all can enjoy them. More and more

Portrait photographs of this family are attractively combined with fish sculpture and a photograph of the family hobby. Daughters' portrait photographs capture their childhood charms forever. As the children grow up and change, the photographs will become more valuable to the family.

A large portrait photograph above a sofa gives personality to this room. Other smaller photographs are set on sliding tracks in a wall unit. The new, lively, relaxed portraits of today fit in well with casual living.

homeowners are learning that well-presented photographs can add a touch of seasoning that will perk up any room.

Although pictures perform many magical decorating tricks, there is no magic in the proper selection of pictures for your home. The pictures you hang should be the pictures you like. Housewives and writers often have a common problem—how to fill that big blank space in front of them. For writers, it's a sheet of paper; for housewives, it's four blank walls in each room of the house.

The solution for both is generally the same: fill the space with what pleases *you* and it will probably please others. However, just as the writer must follow the rules of grammar, so must the home decorator follow rules on the selection and use of pictures. These rules are discussed throughout the book along with different applications of the rules. By studying the ideas presented in this book and making use of those that will fit well into your home, your decorating will have a family flavor, and not one fostered by an interior decorator. By doing this, you will make your photo-decorating projects a matter of family

pride and the difference between what is purely a residence—house or apartment—and a home.

Family pictures can play an important role in a home, providing a running account of the growth and activities of the family. It is desirable that the reader hang one or two pictures in some prominent spot as soon as he has them, rather than putting it off until a later time. Once you procrastinate, the pictures go back into the dresser and desk drawers. On the other hand, you will find if you get one or two pictures up, it is almost certain that others will follow. The more pictures you have on tasteful display, the more they will be enjoyed and the house will feel "lived in" by the family.

Naturally, you are proud of your pictures, and want to show them to their best advantage. A good picture deserves to be properly hung and it will certainly be appreciated more when arranged in such a way that it is easily viewed and adds interest to wall space and furniture groupings.

If you are a one-picture-to-a-wall type of person, it's time you changed your ways. Few things can do more to create a "furnished" look in a room than pictures—but lots of them are needed. When movie producers want to show real desolation they almost invariably shoot a scene of an old cabin or cottage with one lone picture hanging in the room, usually high on the wall—and that does the trick!

Pictures can change the physical appearance of a room. Color, framing and shape are all influencing factors. Pictures need not be great technical masterpieces, but they should be smartly matted and framed. **Any** picture can hang in **most** room settings. Don't be afraid to hang a modernistic picture in an early American setting. Appropriate framing, mounting, or matting can unify your pictures with the decorative scheme of the room. Some appropriateness, however, should be striven for. Very personal pictures or mementoes, such as religious subjects and snapshots, are usually hung in bedrooms, hallways, or dens. More general subjects, such as landscapes or portraits, are better for living and dining areas.

CHAPTER 2

Arranging And Placing Your Pictures

PLACING PICTURES

Pictures can be hung in any room of your home including kitchen and bathroom. They can be hung singly, in pairs, or in large groupings. The first rule of good picture hanging is to look before you hang. Study the wall on which the picture will hang. If it's a large wall space, don't hang one tiny picture; use a large picture or several small ones. Then use the single small picture for a small wall area.

Picture groupings serve many purposes. They can be used to focus interest in an area of the room; to achieve a balanced look in the decor; to highlight a large piece of furniture; to introduce a needed color accent; or to point up a decorative scheme.

Here is something you can do as an aid to placing pictures in a group for a certain wall space. Cut a piece of paper to fit the available space on the wall. If you don't have one sheet of paper large enough, cut several pieces and tape them together. One of the easiest places to get some large sheets of paper would be at the meat market.

Lay the paper on the floor. Then arrange and rearrange the pictures to be hung in this space, moving them around on the paper until the desired effect is gained. For a large grouping, start

with one important picture, the "key" picture (which will usually be the largest one), and build your arrangement around it. The key picture does not have to be in the middle; it may be on the top or on the bottom of the grouping. Proceed to arrange your secondary pictures around the key picture until you get a pleasing effect.

The problem of a window without a view is successfully solved here. By completely surrounding the viewless window with colorful, framed pictures, an artificial scene is created within the room. Framed pictures of different sizes and shapes are grouped around the draped window to draw the eye away from the outside view and focus attention on the room setting as a whole.

Avoid spreading the pictures too far apart, or crowding them too close together. Each should have enough light and space to show to best advantage. A relatively narrow space between pictures will tend to give the feeling of one mass rather than of several separate pictures.

Try to balance the entire grouping so that the eye flows smoothly from one picture to another. Toward this end, the grouping should have a definite "pattern". This will depend on the size of the wall area and the number of pictures. Many times the bottom line of the grouping should be even to unify the group. In special cases, such as grouping around a wall map, the group is arranged in a circle. Use your ingenuity and creativity by adding non-photographic decorations as a part of the grouping;

Let your children's toys add to the decor of their rooms. An informal photo mount such as this toy drum helps solve the problem of what to do with your pictures. By hanging from the ceiling, it is kept out of the way of an active child. Such a clever mount is sure to enchant the heart of every child. He will be delighted to see something of his own being used to decorate the room and the room will become personalized.

punctuating the group in this way will help to relieve the occasional monotony of grouped pictures.

After you have decided on the final grouping, draw the outlines of the pictures on the paper, marking the spot where the nails or hooks will go. Tape the paper to the wall space long enough to mount the hooks or nails, then remove the paper and hang the pictures.

As in hanging single pictures, the choice and placement of a grouping should be related to the wall space available and the furniture beneath it, rather than floating about on the wall alone. Over a sofa, try a large picture or grouping of pictures that fills the space above it. Pictures also can be hung between windows, around windows, over a buffet, chest, or headboard, in a corner and up a stair wall, to mention some possibilities.

Remember that relatively few persons in urban areas have homes whose windows frame a beautifully landscaped vista or an area of natural beauty. For the majority, pictures are the means of providing these vistas and supplying needed color accents as well.

Don't overlook the possibility of a chance to mount or frame personal mementoes and other items and include them in the decor along with photographs. Each can complement the other and give greater interest to the group. Groups of pictures on a wall can be very tastefully highlighted with statues, wall brackets, stuffed animals, lavaboes, figurines, lamps, or planters.

Informal arrangements can be in good taste, depending on where they are placed. In a hallway, for instance, you can hang pictures from the baseboard right up to the ceiling. "Paper" a back stairway with some personal magazine or newspaper clippings, inexpensively framed. Photos of flowers go well in the bathroom, and still-lifes of fruit or food are suitable for the dining area. Photos of food can also be used to "humanize" the kitchen. Informal photos are especially recommended over a fireplace in a bedroom or den. A child's room can be decorated effectively with family pictures, hung along with some of the child's own art work to evoke a sense of pride from the younger members of the family. Don't make the mistake of hanging your

How satisfying it is to keep a picture record of children. Years pass so quickly—the little girl becomes a bride, the boy becomes a man. The arrangement on the next page shows a son's photos from six months to manhood.

Each arrangement needs a point of interest. Whenever possible, the picture or picture grouping should be related to a piece of furniture rather than be isolated. In this case an organ is used as the base for the pictures on the wall behind it. A piece of furniture—couch, chair, or table—can serve to anchor the picture group and give it a feeling of coherence. Colorful ribbons help tie each individual picture into the group. All pictures are uniformly matted and framed; the small molding of the frame does not detract from the pictures but serves to complement them.

Note also how the group is tied together by skillful placement of the pictures according to the angle of the head and body. It is very necessary that the pictures on the outside of the group face toward the center of the group. If any of the subjects faced away from the group, the continuity of composition would be broken. And the pictures are placed so as to be easily viewed at eye level while standing.

HAMMOND

Portrait photographs can be used to beautify the fashionable living room by complementing the decor in many ways. First of all, the picture or grouping should be related in size to the furniture and amount of wall space. A small picture alone is out of scale with a large chair or wall space. On the other hand, large rooms and large furniture will take life-size pictures or large groupings.

In the version seen here there is a combination of a large picture and a grouping of smaller ones. The life size picture creates a dramatic effect, as it is related to the available wall space and to the furniture beneath it. Since it is a large picture, it is necessary to view it from a distance; be sure, therefore, to hang the center of the picture at eye-level from where you will view it. Placement will vary from room to room, but it is always better to hang a picture too low rather than too high.

A grouping of smaller pictures could also fit comfortably into the same room, as illustrated in another example. The photographs are framed in one size and hung in an even row to make a decorative band around a corner. This creates a focal point for a "conversation corner." The group is hung low, just above the corner table and the end of the couch. It is illuminated evenly by the table lamp, while the large picture is well lighted by the overhead illumination.

Emphasis is kept on the pictures by eliminating any clutter on the table, and by using a simple lamp, since they are a part of the group. Placing the lamp in the corner prevents any of the pictures being hidden from view.

In the relaxed portraits below, all lines of composition tend to carry the eye toward the group, not away from it. Whenever possible, it is best to have all photos on the side placed with the subjects facing toward the group.

No matter what means you choose to display your pictures, you'll find they give your den or family room a new warmth and coziness. The focal point for the grouping is a wall map. It is surrounded by pictures of children in the family. This personalizes the "office" area of the home. By mounting small as well as large pictures on the wall, you can save the desk top from a clutter of stand-up photos.

As demonstrated, it is not necessary to put pictures in a frame in order to display them effectively. Those shown at the right are all mounted on a hard board, flush with the edge; all pictures are trimmed to produce a "bleed" edge (no border) for simplicity and uniformity of mounting. Angle of view of the subject is toward the circle and not away from it. Various-sized pictures are placed in what might seem like a haphazard fashion, but they form a casual circle to lead the eye to the group. Part of the desk serves as a baseline for the picture group, giving it a feeling of belonging.

Plain or nearly plain walls make the best background for pictures—though not all plain walls need a picture. By using plain frames on a plain wall, you can give emphasis to decorative furnishings.

Family photos may be hung together successfully and tastefully as a grouping, even though the group may contain all ages and the pictures may be in such shapes as ovals, horizontals, verticals, or other odd designs. Just remember to hang the pictures with a definite base line, for unity, and to place the group at eye level, or slightly lower.

BOSTON

children's pictures too high. Hang pictures level with the children's line of sight; they will appreciate your thoughtfulness.

Try to allow a relatively narrow space between the pictures. This narrow space gives the feeling of one picture and helps to tie them together as a group. On the other hand, don't crowd the pictures. Use your own judgment and place them so that each picture has enough light and space to show off to best advantage.

If you're hanging a picture or a grouping over a sofa or couch, the pictures should in nearly all cases be centered over the furniture below it, thereby making it an integral part of the group. Also place the pictures at least six to eight inches from the top of the sofa so that a seated person's head will not touch the frames.

A successful display of pictures need not be costly, and can be made successfully even in a cramped apartment. Cluttered and haphazard groupings, or single pictures with untidy surroundings will cause a loss of interest in each picture as well as in the total artistic appeal. Rows and stacks of pictures arranged without system are also distracting.

LEARN DECORATING TRICKS

Since a room, like a costume, can be given distinction with well-chosen accessories, the "do-it-yourself" decorator should familiarize himself with some of the decorating tricks that can be accomplished with pictures. A favorite picture can provide the color scheme for a room, but often amateur decorators do not know how to do this.

Many people lack confidence in their ability to select pictures for their homes. They may "know what they like" but may not be sure that it is right for them. Most people react strongly to color; yet there is a great difference in reactions. Some cannot distinguish differences in hue and tone, while others can detect the most subtle combinations of colors. Still others have little understanding of a huge range of color harmonies.

Any person with a natural aptitude for color can develop ability to appreciate a work of art through a better understanding of color harmony. One can learn to appraise variations in tone and quality by making a conscious effort to recognize the various

Pictures which are similar in some way—in subject, color, or method of composition—may be grouped together successfully. These can be tied together as a group by simple framing and methods of display. The version shown below uses the angle of view of the subjects as a basis for a unique display. The subject for the grouping is the same young man shown at various stages of his early childhood; an arrow-like design was used to connect the angles of view and form a composition. Light frames on a dark background complement the decor.

Informal pictures conform easily to the mood of a family room or den, especially when they are combined with trophies, plaques or other mementoes of the favorite family sport. Large rooms such as these are especially suitable to large pictures, as well as groupings of several small pictures.

The large pictures in the photo above are centered over the piece of furniture underneath, while in the panel grouping, which is not centered, the placement is balanced by a large plant. Always use a vertical picture where vertical lines are suggested or needed. Pictures and other furnishings should seem to belong together. In this case, the large, vertical picture complements the "movie house billboard" type panel to fill the available wall space and harmonize with the decor. The billboard type of panel is a good way to display family photos collected over the years, since they often come in assorted sizes and shapes. This is a neat way to keep a grouping from looking splattered on a wall.

These pictures are effectively displayed in a dining area. One of the pictures completely covers one cabinet door for an unusual mounting.

relationships of colors. If the pictures are given careful study, it is easy to call attention to the best features of a picture and use them to show off your furnishings to best advantage.

Pictures can change the physical appearance of a room. Color, framing, and shape are all factors. A long wall can be made to look shorter, for example, by use of a horizontal, panel type picture. A horizontal picture hung low will make a low ceiling appear *higher,* while a vertical picture hung fairly high tends to bring a ceiling *down.* A receding color such as blue makes a room or hall look longer, while a "forward" color such as red at the end of a long room tends to foreshorten it. A very small picture should be hung low over an appropriate piece of furniture so that it doesn't look lost.

PICTURES GIVE A ROOM DISTINCTION

Always think of pictures as the easiest means of adding life, color and sparkle to a room. Pictures will do more than any other accessory to give a room charm and distinction, since they are not only decorative in themselves, but also "open up" the bare walls of a room and provide a place for the eyes to rest.

Remember that today's living habits discourage collections of photos leaning on desks, tables and piano. Most people want decorative objects that are functional as well. Used on walls or to accent shelves, open cupboards and the like, photos fit into the casual pattern of today's living.

In the new homes with their open planning, room dividers often are used to separate living and dining areas. Pictures can be used to advantage on these dividers, along with greenery and sculpture. If the divider is open, two pictures of the same size may be hung back to back so that the effect will be attractive from either side.

It is not necessary that every picture be hung, and pictures may be used very effectively to punctuate bookshelves and other areas. Several colorful and handsomely framed smaller pictures placed on chests or tables add to the individuality of a room. Hang pictures in unexpected places. If the picture is interesting

and well-framed, it will add spice to a room. Pictures are meant to be **enjoyed,** and what better way to do this than by placing them where they can be easily viewed! Become picture conscious and don't be stingy, but don't crowd them; spread them out low and high, widely and handsomely. They can work for you and become a medium of expressive design.

CHAPTER 3

Simple Ways to Display Small Pictures

Over the holidays and during the summer months the snapshots will really accumulate. An end-of-vacation inventory of pictures taken may yield an impressive collection.

A few of these, along with some professionally made portraits, will be mailed off to family and friends, while others will find a home in an album—but what about those lying loose in the drawers? Why not put them to constructive use? With a few inexpensive props they can be brought out of the drawers and put where they will be seen, converted into personalized gifts. Some of the possibilities are shown on the following pages.

In keeping with today's trend of informal living, snapshots, as well as larger portraits, can be displayed effectively as well as inexpensively. As in contemporary frames for the pictures, basically simple designs are prevalent.

As you turn from chapter to chapter in this book you will readily realize that here are some simple ideas which you can use to display your own pictures for everyone to enjoy. Some of the applications and possibilities for smaller pictures are shown on these pages.

Milk Carton Paperweight

A solid square paperweight which will hold down Dad's business papers or Grandmother's clippings is made from the bottom part of a clean, quart-size milk carton.

First cut the carton down on three sides, to a height equal to the width, leaving the fourth side with an extra flap in this same length. Fill the carton with sand or any other weighty substance. Then bend the long side down to make a top and complete the cube. Bind the top and sides together with colorful tape, while at the same time attaching photos on all sides, the tape serving as border for the pictures.

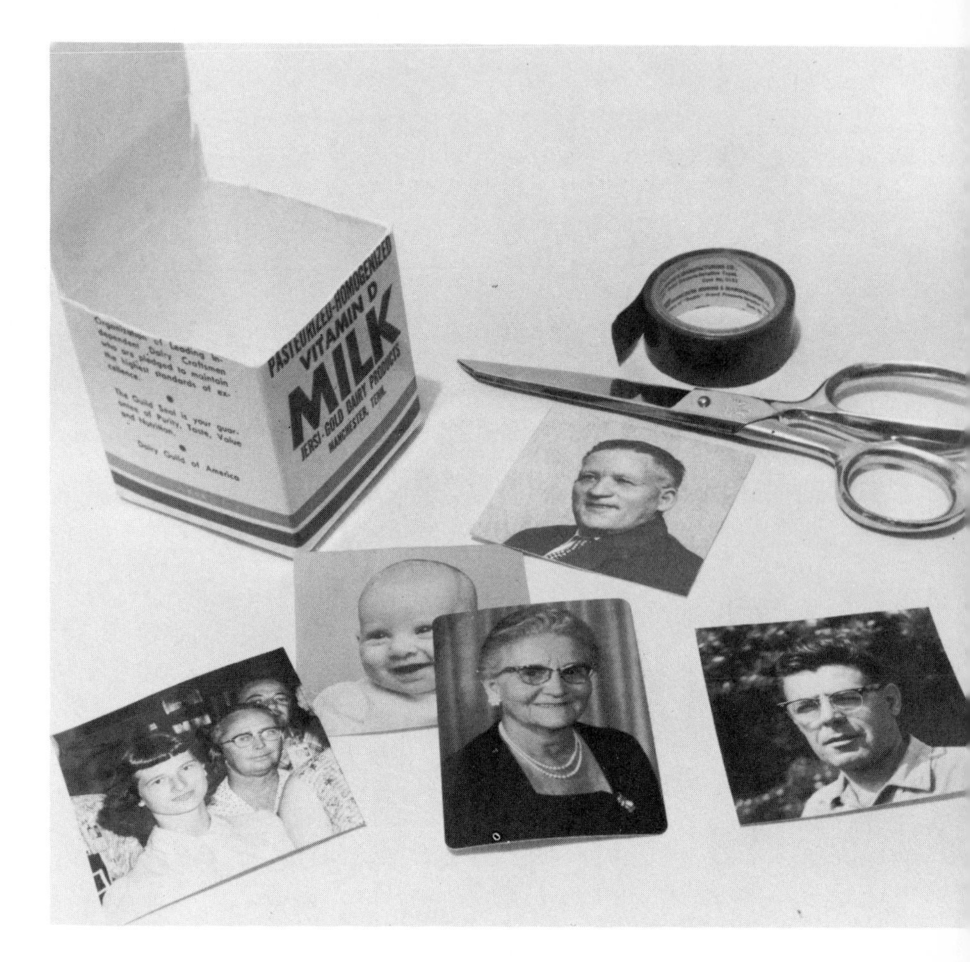

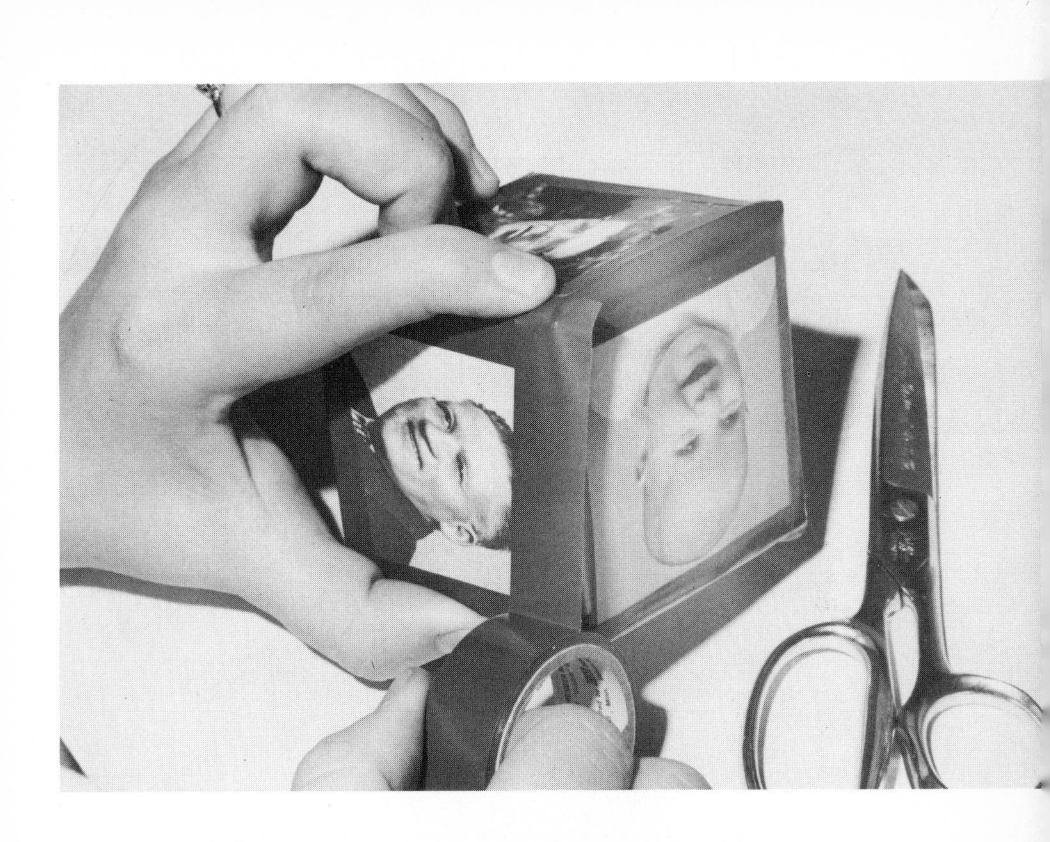

Paperweight and Letter Box

A clear glass paperweight may be decorated with portraits or snapshsots trimmed to fit the underside and taped with clear tape face-up to the glass.

Letter or stationery boxes may be made from a shoebox lined and covered with colorful art paper. The boxes are personalized by trimming with snapshots cut in fancy designs.

Photo Stands

Shown here are three methods of displaying small, unframed photos so they may stand alone. On the left is a book holder called Holz All. It is adjustable and will hold small, mounted prints successfully.

A strip of cardboard taped to the back holds one of the prints, while a bent hairpin in another works in much the same way. Any of these methods keeps down the clutter by allowing the picture to be free-standing, rather than precariously propped against some knickknack.

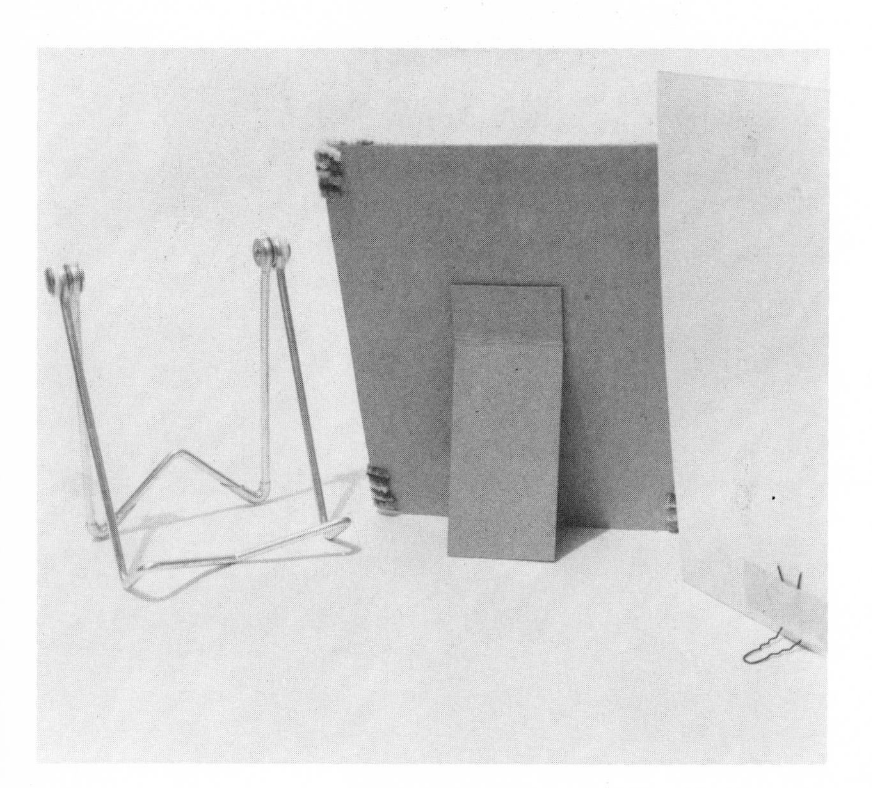

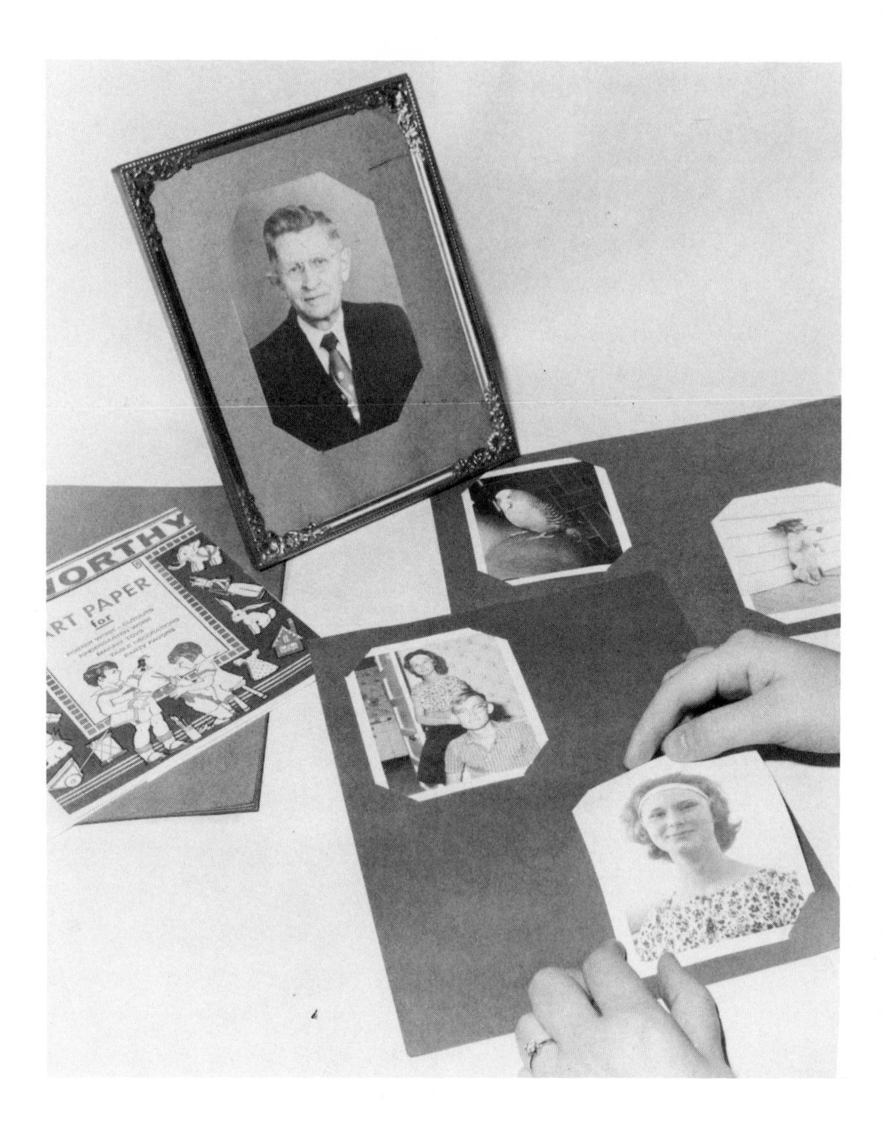
ART PAPER
for

Quick Mounts

Snapshots are much more attractive and can be displayed more effectively when mounted. Here is a simple and inexpensive method.

Buy a package of art or construction paper at the dime store and select the color sheet you prefer. In selecting colors, many will prefer the mounts made of the conventional black, brown, tan, and gray paper; but try to experiment with the brighter shades, you will like them. Red, in particular, is very effective.

Next, cut a pattern from stiff paper or cardboard to the exact size of your print. Trim a ½ inch triangle off each corner of this pattern. Now lay the pattern exactly in the center of the colored mount and make a cut with a sharp razor blade in the mount across where each corner was cut off the pattern. Insert the corners of your print into these slots—presto, your print is mounted.

Several prints may be mounted on one sheet. One package of paper will mount many pictures and add much to their attractiveness. These can either be displayed informally just as they are, or they can be mounted on stiff board and placed in a frame.

"Fuzzy Frame"

A very inexpensive way to mount small pictures and keep them out of a drawer is a "fuzzy picture frame" made of pipe cleaners. First, cut out a piece of cardboard about ¾ inch larger than the picture and paste or dry mount the picture in the center of the cardboard. Then select and place pipe cleaners in the border around the print. Packages of multicolor pipe cleaners are available for 25c. Any combination of colors may be used. It is a simple matter to glue the cleaners in place, bending over the ends to wrap around the back. A piece of cardboard folded and pasted to the back will form an easel support for the frame.

Match Books

Personalized match-book covers are fun to make. Just paste the photograph on the outside of a commercial book of matches, after trimming to fit, and you will have a nice, inexpensive gift for family and friends.

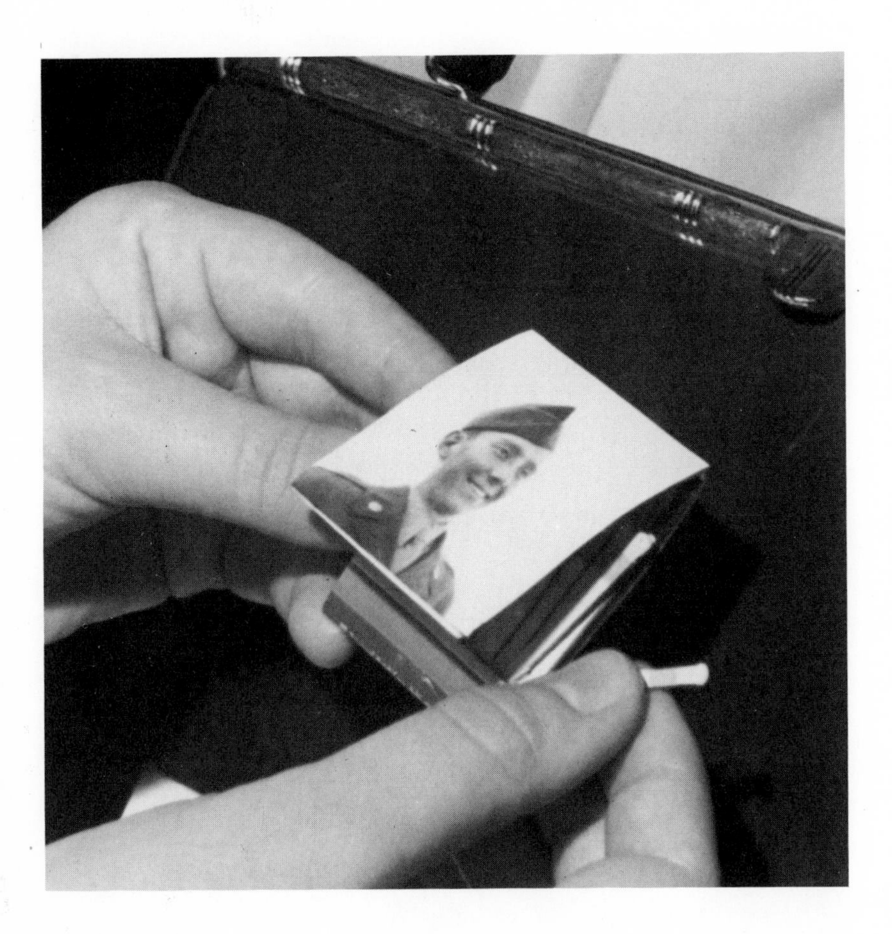

Stand-Up Mount

Whenever possible you should use your own imagination to mount your small pictures in unusual ways. Use objects other than the usual type of mount, and you'll find they can be eye-catchers. In the case below, a baby's toy telephone rattle made a good stand-up mount for the baby's picture. The picture was cut out and taped to the toy at the back.

Macaroni Decorates Miniature Frame

You can make your own miniature picture frames like the one shown below from materials already on hand. You will need a top from a plastic food container and several pieces of uncooked elbow macaroni. The corner sections of macaroni are glued around the front edge to make a decorative design. After the glue has dried, spray paint the frame gold. The picture is glued into the circle inside the top. A piece of cardboard taped or glued to the back acts as a stand for the frame.

The photos below and opposite illustrate other "no-cost" ways of mounting small portraits or snapshots on stand-up frames. Three different ways of using aluminum foil as a background mat for mounting photos are shown: First, a cardboard back is cut a little larger than the picture to be mounted. Then the foil is fitted over the cardboard, conforming to the various shapes.

Another photo shows how you can use plain white cardboard as a backing for pictures. Ordinary cardboard such as that used as stiffeners for men's shirts will do, and the frames can be stepped up by adding various "appliques," such as the stars shown below.

The heart-shaped picture is mounted on a red heart cut from art paper.

Such variations give you a chance to use your imagination. Let your mind soar!

One photo shows three different ways of using aluminum foil as a background mat for mounting photos. First, cut a pattern from a piece of paper in the shape or design which suits the particular picture. The shape may be square, round, oval, or many other different forms. To add variety you may cut the edges in scallops or other designs. Next, place the pattern on a piece of cardboard and cut around the edge. Then fit the foil over the cardboard, conforming to the various shapes.

CHAPTER 4

Ways Of Mounting Pictures

All pictures can be quickly and securely mounted by either of two general methods: dry mounting or wet mounting.

Dry mounting is the fastest, safest and easiest method, and has long been the most widely used process for photographs. It is a process whereby you can mount your prints without the use of messy paste, glue, or cement. To mount any material by the dry mounting process, two things are required: a method of producing heat under pressure (a thermostatically controlled electric press for large quantities, or an ordinary household electric iron for small photos), and dry mounting tissue. The dry mounting press is a simple piece of electrically-operated equipment which applies heat and pressure. The dry mounting tissue is a thin sheet of paper, similar to a sheet of waxed paper, which is coated on both sides with a coating of very high-grade thermoplastic adhesive. When heat and pressure are applied to the dry mounting tissue, the adhesive is activated and, upon cooling, it forms a very strong bond with the material to which it has been applied. The average print can be dry mounted in a matter of a few seconds and there is no mess to clean up when you are finished.

Modern day electric dry mounting presses are equipped with the very latest thermostatic heat controls and automatic timing devices, and even the most inexperienced person can turn out perfect dry mounted prints that **remain** perfectly mounted for years.

They do not normally curl or buckle due to atmospheric changes and no deposit is left that could attract insects.

Should you plan to un-mount a print for any reason, be sure to mount it with Fotoflat Tissue, a product of Seal, Inc. of Shelton, Connecticut. Materials which have been mounted with this tissue can be removed very easily by the re-application of heat. Materials subject to rather high temperatures should not be mounted with Fotoflat.

MOUNT BOARDS

A smooth finish white board works out most satisfactorily for dry mounting; as do the pebble-grained type of boards used for mats. Never use a clay finish board (the type of board used by sign painters). A reaction occurs between the adhesive and the clay filler in this type of board and very unsatisfactory mounting results. There are any number of concerns which supply inexpensive mount boards; addresses may be obtained from Seal, Inc., which manufactures the dry mounting presses and tissues.

MOISTURE IN MOUNT BOARDS AND PRINTS

The most common cause of bubbles and blisters is moisture in the mount board or print. A good rule to follow is to heat the mount board and print with the iron or press for a minute or two prior to using it. If you do not first drive out the moisture, a vapor or steam may occur during the mounting operation. Since the tissue is moisture-proof, a pocket of vapor or steam will be trapped between the mount board and the tissue, creating the bubbles or blisters. There is very little that can be done to eliminate these bubbles once the material is mounted. In really humid weather *always* pre-heat prior to mounting.

Another cause of bubbles is operating the iron or press at too high a temperature. The hotter it is, the greater the possibility of steam or vapor forming from the moisture in the mount board. Therefore, always operate your heat source at the lowest possible temperature setting that will produce a satisfactory job. Too much heat is much worse than not enough heat. You can always put the print back under the press and re-mount it if the press wasn't hot enough the first time. There is very little, however, that can be done to save a print that was mounted with an overheated press.

A weight should be placed on the freshly mounted print immediately upon removing it from the press; this will eliminate curling of the mounted print and board during cooling.

Either single or double weight prints can be dry mounted successfully. Attach a sheet of dry mounting tissue to the back of the print by lining them both up as accurately as possible and tacking them together in a single spot at the center of the tissue. Allow the corners to be free and use only the edge or tip of the iron. Trim the tissue and print together. The tissue should be exactly the same size as the print or just a little larger so that the tissue can be lined up with at least two edges of the print to eliminate extra trimming. The print is then ready to be placed on the mount or mounting board.

Since the tissue is not sticky, you can place the print just where you want it on the mount. When you have positioned the picture correctly, you can "tack" it onto the mount board by lifting the corners of the print and touching the tip of the iron to the tissue, which will seal the tissue to the mount. By "tacking" the print to the mount board in this manner you will prevent the print from moving out of position when you place the print and mount in the press, or when you place your iron on it. Always place a clean sheet of paper over the face of the print before placing it in the press to prevent the face of the print from being impregnated with any dirt. In using a household iron, cover the print with a piece of paper and iron the print evenly all over; starting from the center, gradually press out to the edges, holding the iron in each area long enough to mount it.

MODERN PRINT DISPLAY PANELS

To effectively display informal family photos or salon type pictures, cover an unused window or door or a blank wall with a piece of inexpensive soft wallboard material. Painted a light gray or pastel color, it makes an outstanding background for both mounted and unmounted prints. Ordinary household straight pins, cut short so they will not go all the way through the board, can be used to fasten prints to the board. Don't put the pins through the prints or mount board, but rather right up against the edge of it. They are hardly noticeable and are much better looking than ordinary thumbtacks.

MAKING A PRINT MOUNTING—RULE FOR CENTERING

Prints can be placed in the exact center of a mount easily and quickly with a cardboard rule such as the one shown. It consists of a two-inch strip of cardboard with two scales drawn on the edges, starting at zero in the center and extending in both directions. To use, place the print on the mount, then place the rule on top of the print and adjust both the print and the mount until opposite edges line up with identical markings on the rule. There will then be an equal margin on both sides of the print. The same procedure is used to establish the top and bottom margins.

WET MOUNTING

Rubber cement has many advantages as a mounting agent. The print is held smooth and flat and tends not to wrinkle. Surplus cement is easily removed from the mount when dry by light rubbing with a cloth. The problem of handling a quickly drying paste is done away with. At a later time, the print may be removed easily and safely for remounting.

The do-it-yourselfer may want to mix a solution that maintains the strong points of rubber cement and to a great extent eliminates its faults, especially the possibility of the print curling when it is dry. Mix a solution of Knox gelatin about a third stronger than the recipe on the package. Apply this while warm to the back of the prints with a sponge or cloth. Allow the prints to curl (as they will) until dry. Then straighten with a straight-edge or in a press. When mounted, these prints will not curl and pull loose from the mount.

Center the print on the mount and outline lightly with pencil. First spread the cement evenly and thinly around the edges, up to the lines on the mount. When the edge is finished, the surplus cement is quickly spread over the central portions of the space. The back of the print is then treated in the same manner. One very important point to remember is **not to spread cement at the corners of either the mount or the print:** always leave a triangle about ¼ inch in size.

Dry the surfaces about one minute—never much longer. Best results are obtained if the cement is tacky when the contact is made. Carefully attach one edge of the print, preferably the longer side. Rub this edge into contact with a cloth or squeegee roller. Hold the print in a curve while it is gradually brought into contact with the mount. For best contact roll the entire print with a squeegee. Great care should be exercised in removing all air bubbles between the picture and mount and making certain that the corners are firmly glued (take a brush and carefully apply a very thin film of mucilage, paste or glue to the corners). The print may then be placed in a press or gently pounded with the fist for a short time. Thus mounted, a print will rarely buckle or warp and it cannot peel off the mount at the corners.

A small square of wire screening about 2 x 2″ clamped in an ordinary spring-type clothes pin makes an excellent applicator for spreading rubber cement over the prints or mounts.

SPRAY ADHESIVE

A versatile new spray adhesive that can be used to make either temporary or permanent bonds is now available from the Retail Tape and Gift Wrap division of 3M Company.

The new product, called **3M Spra-Ment adhesive,** is ideal for a number of photographic applications, including photo mounting.

Spra-Ment features a much higher solid content than was previously available in an aerosol can, making for a much more aggressive adhesive, preventing soak through in use with most materials. It is fast drying, colorless, and heat and water resistant. The adhesive is non-curling and non-staining and provides excellent adhesion with paper, cloth, cardboard, many plastic films, metal foil, glass and most painted surfaces. It is almost

invisible when applied and will not wrinkle paper or other thin materials, and is highly resistant to embrittlement and other forms of film degradation.

The versatile adhesive may be used in three different techniques for a variety of applications. For non-permanent bonds, a light coat of Spra-Ment is applied to one surface and allowed to dry at least five minutes before mounting. Surfaces then can be separated when desired without adhesive transfer. For permanent bonds on such porous materials as paper or cardboard, one surface is coated and bonds are made while the adhesive is wet and aggressively tacky. For permanent bonds on non-porous materials, such as metal foil or plastic films, both surfaces are coated and allowed a minimum of one minute to dry before assembly.

CHAPTER 5

Use Mats To Perk Up Your Pictures

Imaginative matting can change an ordinary framed picture into an eye-catcher. Mats are used to call attention artfully to the picture, to separate the picture from the frame and background, and provide a rest space which actually strengthens the lines or colors of the picture.

The single professional portrait on the next page is a dramatic accent in the family room. It illustrates the trend toward impressive-sized family photographs in the manner of oil paintings of earlier days. The simple frame and colored mat help to emphasize the picture.

The type of mount used in the illustration is the type most commonly used for portraits. A window is cut in the mat, usually beveled (at an angle); this bevel may be gilded or painted a suitable color when it is desirable to introduce an accent or a note of contrast.

Mats are usually cut from boards made for this purpose, but cardboard or fiberboard with a pebbled or textured surface is also used. These most frequently are white, off-white, pale gray or beige in color. Recently, colored mats have become popular. Almost any color may be used, provided it harmonizes with the picture, the frame, the wall or the other furnishings in the room.

Variety can be achieved in many ways. When special colors are desired, the mat can be colored to match with water color or paint. Custom mats can be made by covering them with a

variety of materials. Eye-appeal for your pictures may be achieved by using rough linen, calico, velvet, decorator's burlap, raw silk, metal foil, straw matting, wallpaper, or any other material you like that fits in with the decorating theme and the theme of the picture. A variety of colors may be used, as well as stripes, plaids, or checks.

MAT CUTTER

A new mat cutter on the market is a worthwhile photo accessory. The Dexter Mat Cutter (made by Russell Harrington Cutlery Co. of Southbridge, Mass.) is an ingenious cutting instrument for making any size opening you desire in a photo mount. All too often when you want to mount your darkroom masterpiece you find that all you can get in the way of mounts is the standard 16 x 20 board with standard 8 x 10, 11 x 14 or 14 x 17 openings. Ownership of this cutter will permit you to cut just the size opening which will best frame your picture. Its adjustable blade allows you to vary the depth of cut as well as the angle.

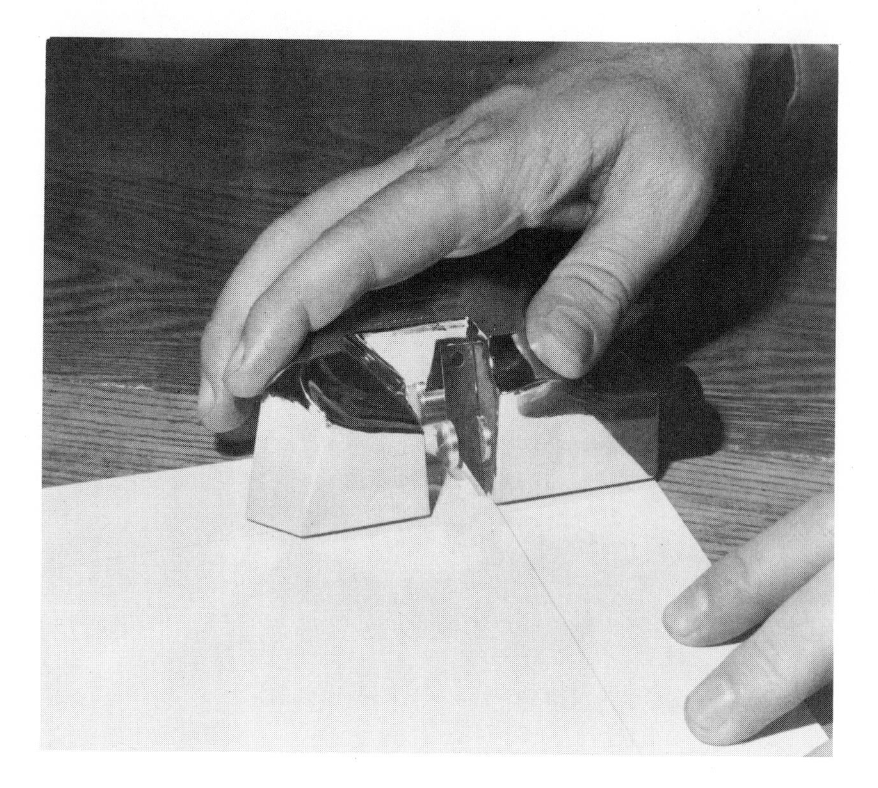

To prepare a mat or cardboard for cutting, draw light pencil lines on the mat as a guide. The outline should be slightly smaller than the edges of the picture (not including the border). The blade is adjusted to the desired angle and depth and locked in position. A T-square or a steel straight edge is then placed parallel to the guide line and the mat cutter is drawn against the straight edge to make the cut.

VACATION PHOTOS

An effective way of displaying your prized vacation pictures is to frame and hang them in a wall grouping in the den or family room. A unique background mat was made for these pictures from road maps. The mood is set at a glance for the viewer. When unusual mats such as this are used it is best to use simple frames, so that the frame will not detract from the picture and mat.

The width of mats is a matter of taste, and depends primarily on the effect desired. The photo on the next page shows how a narrow-margin mat was used to make an odd-size photograph fit into a standard-size frame. Without this method of mounting, the picture would have required a custom-made frame. The picture was matted and mounted on a standard size board to fit the frame, and the narrow white mat complements the white gloves.

Mats serve still another purpose. A mat can be used to make a very small picture seem larger and give it added importance. A wide-margin mat can be used to dramatize a small picture, especially when it is plain and coupled with a narrow frame. With the right mat almost any picture can be fitted into a picture grouping or used to repeat the color scheme of a room.

Here are some hints on mats from the Picture and Frame Institute: Mats should normally never be less than 2½″ at the top and sides and 3″ at the bottom. This variation in size is designed to compensate for an optical illusion, for a mat exactly the same size on all four sides actually appears to be narrower at the bottom. The wider margin at the bottom adds

visual support. To maintain the proportion in framing a square picture, both the side and top margins should be the same width, while the bottom margin should be slightly larger than those of the top and sides.

A vertical picture looks best when the side margins are narrower than the top margin. The bottom margin of a vertical should be even wider than the top to accent the upward movement of the picture shape. In horizontal pictures, where the movement is from side to side, the top margin should be narrower and the bottom margin wider than the side.

French mats are those having a series of decorative lines around the window. A band of color, repeating one of the colors in the picture, may be painted between two of the lines, or strips of gold or silver foil glued on and mitered at the corners. **Spandrel mats** are those having an oval or round window and may also have a series of colored lines drawn around the window.

In selecting the right mat board for the picture, it should be remembered that pictures with strong lines look best with mats having a pronounced texture. Framed action shots look best with wide mats. Other pictures are given necessary perspective by using two mats which protrude slightly and are either gilded, silvered or painted to add a touch of color.

Acoustical Tile Mat

In this case the photo mount also serves as a mat for the picture. The picture is attached to a square of acoustical tile with glue or rubber cement. Tile is available in several decorative designs. Grooved edges will require trimming with a sharp knife or razor blade around the edge. Pictures can be hung by regular picture frame wire attached to fiber back by tacks, or attached to a standing mount, as shown here.

Mats serve a practical purpose besides helping to accent and enlarge the picture. Due to their thickness they prevent the surface of color prints from coming into contact with the picture glass, on which moisture sometimes condenses. When this happens the picture wrinkles, or the colors may be ruined.

Music Mood Mat

The mood for this picture is set immediately by the mat, made up of pages from song books pasted onto a cardboard back. The picture was mounted in the center, on top of the music. Titles of the songs are visible. The picture is hung at eye level for easier viewing and reading of the titles.

Fabrics on Mats

Perfect for family room or den are these portrait photographs mounted on hardboard covered with felt and decorated with colorful trims. One of the pictures is trimmed with a sailor's rope coiled into an unusual design. The other is trimmed with rick-rack to form a frame. Both are colorful ways of adding items at hand to the mat to produce striking results to show off the portrait photographs—the family's most personal form of art.

Objects on Mats

When cost is a factor, use materials at hand. Imagination and ingenuity have resulted in quite as many spectacular displays as have been developed with expensive labor and materials. Often it is the incongruous touch, the unexpected combination of objects that gives a display a special flair. Here, a baby picture is personalized by adding to the mat symbols of babyhood, diaper pins, in such a way that they frame the photograph. Rubber cement will serve to mount the pins. Rubber cement permits easier removal than glue, should you wish to change the picture in later years.

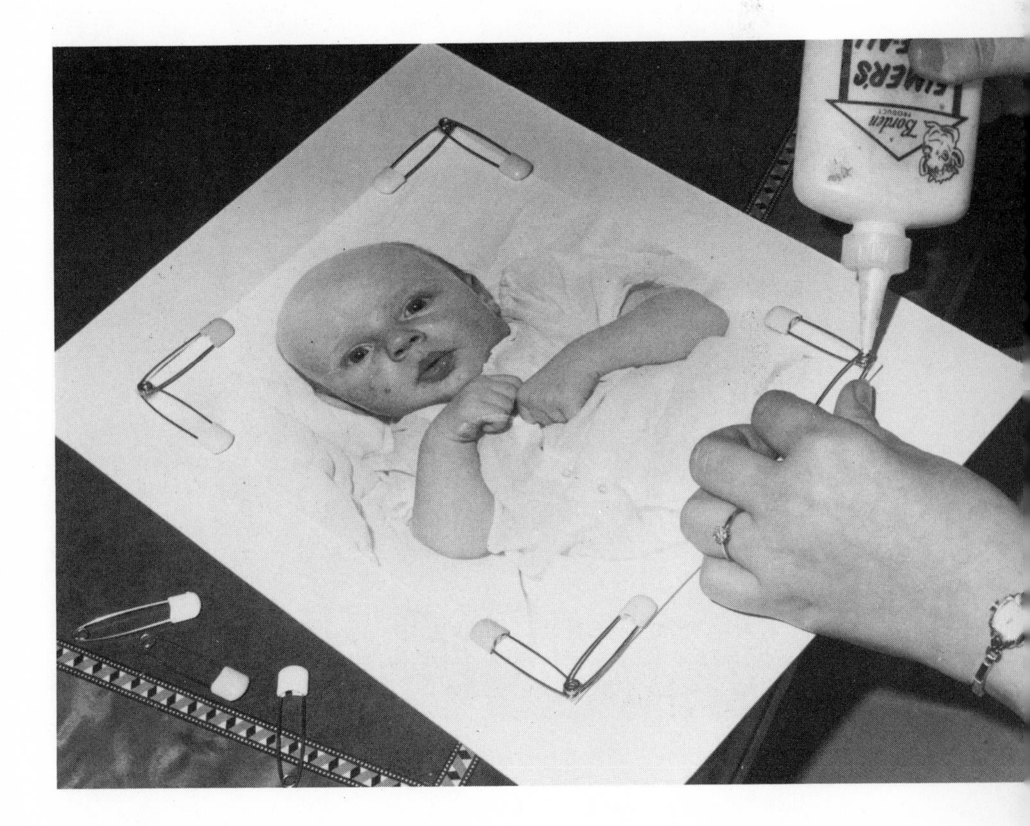

CHAPTER 6

Framing Ideas

Any picture that you place any value on should be under glass. The glass protects it from dirt and damage and greatly increases its brilliance. There is also a consideration of showmanship involved: the use of protecting glass increases the impression of value in the eyes of the beholder.

A frame is naturally required when glass is used, as a means of holding the glass in place. But it has an important pictorial function as well. Along with the mount, it helps create the necessary "isolation" required for the full appreciation of a picture. Like the mount, it must be decidedly subordinate to the picture and relatively inconspicuous.

WHAT A FRAME SHOULD DO

What are some of the functions of a frame besides forming a support for the picture? Here are some of the things, according to the Picture and Frame Institute, that a frame should do:

> A beautiful and suitable frame can transform a very ordinary picture into a work of art.
>
> It should focus attention on the picture and at the same time draw the eye to the center of interest in the picture, possibly by repeating a color in the picture.
>
> It should harmonize in color and weight with the subject matter.

It should contain, but not arrest, the movement of color and line in the picture.

It should, when necessary, create an illusion of depth or size or added perspective.

It should strengthen the composition it frames but never dominate it.

It should provide a transition between the picture and the wall on which it hangs.

Even more important than design, color, or finish are the proportions, or width and depth of a frame. A wide, deep frame emphasizes strong detail in a picture. A busy composition often is enhanced with a complex frame. Strong colors in a picture call for heavier frames. So do architectural subjects, animals and objects denoting strength.

Frames with simple profiles are best for colorful and vigorous subjects. A small picture can be given distinction with a wide, deep frame and an insert in one of the minor colors in the picture.

PICTURE GLASS WITHOUT GLARE

A specially processed glass which eliminates light reflection, yet permits clear visibility from any angle, is adding new beauty to pictures that must be framed with glass. This new glass, called **Tru-site,** is a product of the Dearborn Glass Company.

The new glass has a matte finish that prevents distortion and reveals colors in their true tone values. Pictures framed with this glass can now be hung opposite picture windows or in other locations where daylight or artificial light previously caused a disturbing glare. The secret of this new glass, which is almost invisible, is the finish applied to both sides that reduces surface light reflection to a bare minimum.

The finish is said to be permanent, and the glass can be cut just like ordinary glass. Though somewhat more expensive than regular picture glass, the cost is offset by the added beauty given the picture.

If you are planning to cut a piece of glass to fit a special size frame you will need a clean cardboard-covered table on which to place the glass while cutting. A good way to cut glass is to use a yardstick or other straight edge as a guide. To prevent the yardstick from slipping, drive a nail into the workbench near each end of the ruler so that projecting ends will rest against it.

In cutting, you should hold the glass cutter at a slant and drawn forward, exerting firm but even pressure. After cutting, tap the glass lightly at each end of the cut on the reverse side, while pressing the sheet of glass slightly downward. Do not go over a line more than once and avoid crossing a cut line, since this may break the glass.

Pictures to be framed without glass should be mounted on a fairly heavy mounting board with a smooth surface. As a protection the picture should be sprayed with at least one or two coats of a clear spray. With this coating applied, the picture may be wiped clean of any dust without any effect on the picture.

Every picture is made to be seen in some way, but many never are because space is limited and change-overs in conventional frames are expensive and inconvenient. This type of frame is especially suitable for an office or family room. It is not only an interesting and inexpensive wall decoration, but it also enables you to vary your picture display as fast as you would slip a letter out of and into an envelope.

The multiple frame is made of strips of molding rabbeted on the back side and fastened to the wall. The pictures fit into grooves which are recessed out of the back side of the molding. For this type of display, it is necessary to mount all pictures on a board. (It is designed to take a 20-inch mount.) The pictures can be inserted at the end or, if the mount board is not too stiff, they can be bent slightly and slipped into place without removing all of the pictures. All of your pictures get a chance for display in this multiple frame which allows fast and easy changes.

PADDED PICTURE FRAMES

Those unsightly marks left on walls by picture frames can be easily prevented by gluing felt pads, foam rubber, or upholstery tacks to the back corners of the frame. Pads can be cut from upholstery felt or an old hat and attached near the lower corner. They should be close to the edges, but not so close that they can be seen when the picture is hung. The frame will touch the wall only at these points and will not mark the wall with dust lines around the edges. This will also help the frame to hang straight.

If you would like to hang a picture on an inside brick wall in your home, such as a fireplace wall, try this: Make a small wedge from a piece of soft wood, beveling two sides just enough so the block will drive tightly into the mortar-joint between the bricks. Then attach a small screw at the center of the block and hang the picture on it.

HANGING HEAVY PICTURE FRAMES

It is much easier to hang heavy picture frames if an ordinary table fork is placed over the nail. In this way, the fork handle guides the picture wire to engage the hook.

To keep a picture from slipping and hanging askew, support it on two hooks or nails instead of one. Place them on the wall an inch or so apart. This will keep the wire from dropping down at one corner. Before driving the nails, it's wise to cover the spot with tape to keep the plaster from cracking.

Hang pictures in such a manner that nails, hooks and wires are unseen—the exception is a very large or heavy picture which must be hung with parallel wires attached to a molding. With a round picture, place the wires in an inverted "V" shape; the picture wire still need not be visible above the top of the frame.

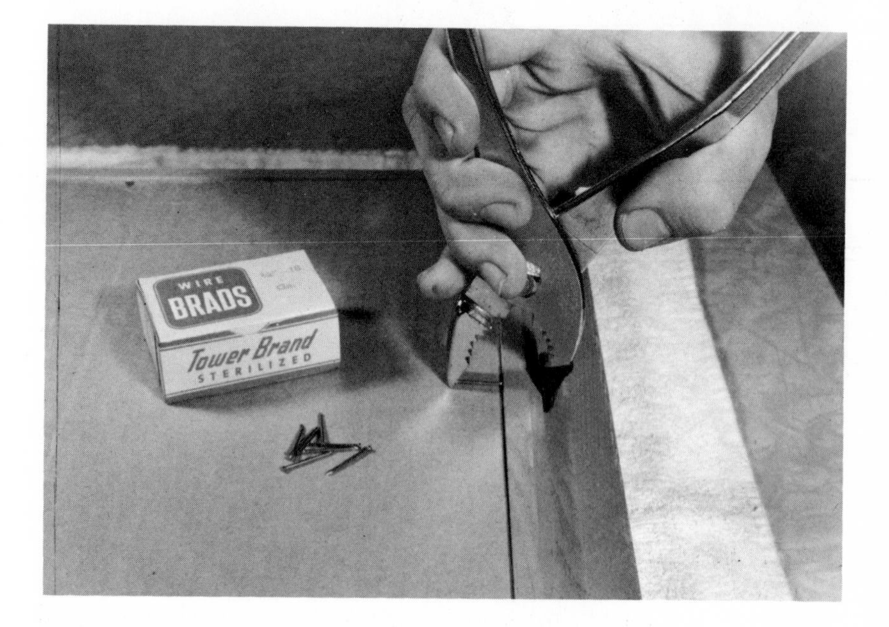

Glaziers' triangular points are ideal for holding a picture in a narrow frame, but the special guns needed to insert the points correctly are too expensive for the occasional framer. Tapping with a hammer often loosens the frame miters. Avoid this by using a more common item—wire brads—to hold the picture and mount board in the frame.

Pliers can be used to secure the backing. (The slip-joint type of pliers are more appropriate than those shown.) Slip a piece of hose over the lower jaw, or wrap with tape, then place the pliers with the padded jaw against the frame. Catch the head of the brad with the other jaw and press into the wood. The brad is driven straight in without bending or splitting the frame.

Here are the steps to use in placing a dust cover on the back of a frame:

Place the frame face down on a work table covered with a towel or soft cloth. Apply glue to the protruding edge around the back opening, and spread evenly as shown.

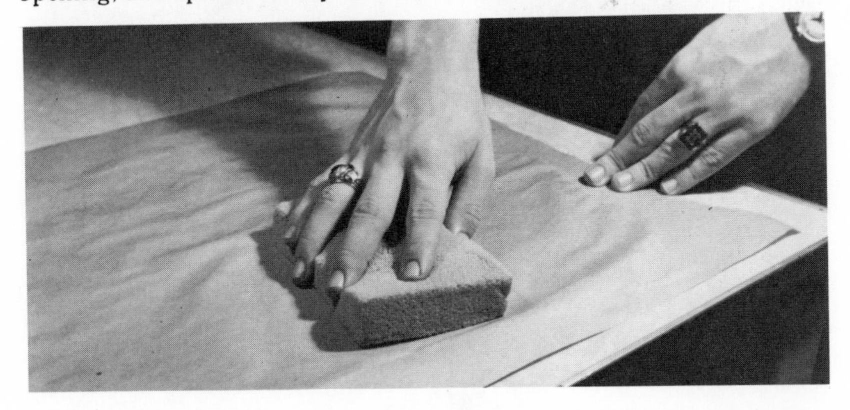

Cut a piece of brown paper which is about three inches larger than the frame all the way around. Place this paper on the table and dampen it lightly all over with a moist sponge.

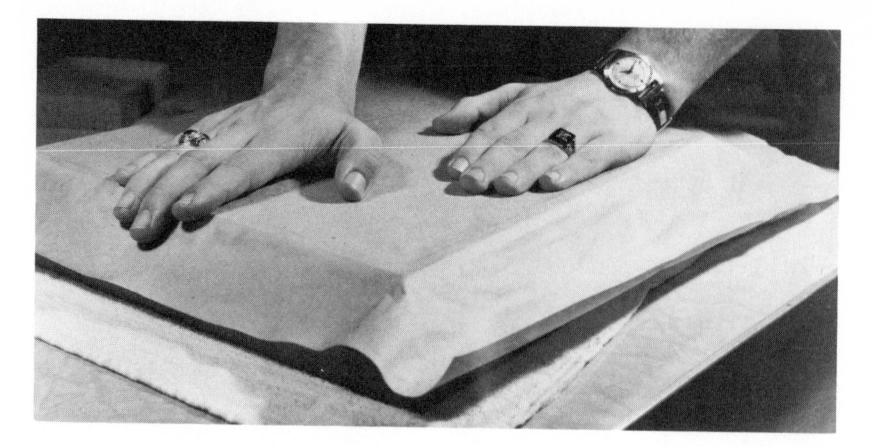

Immediately place the paper over the frame, pressing out all wrinkles with both hands, from the center outward.

As the paper dries it will pull taut with no wrinkles. When the paper is dry, push downward across the edge of the frame with a fine-tooth file or with sandpaper. This sanding will trim the paper off neatly around the edge.

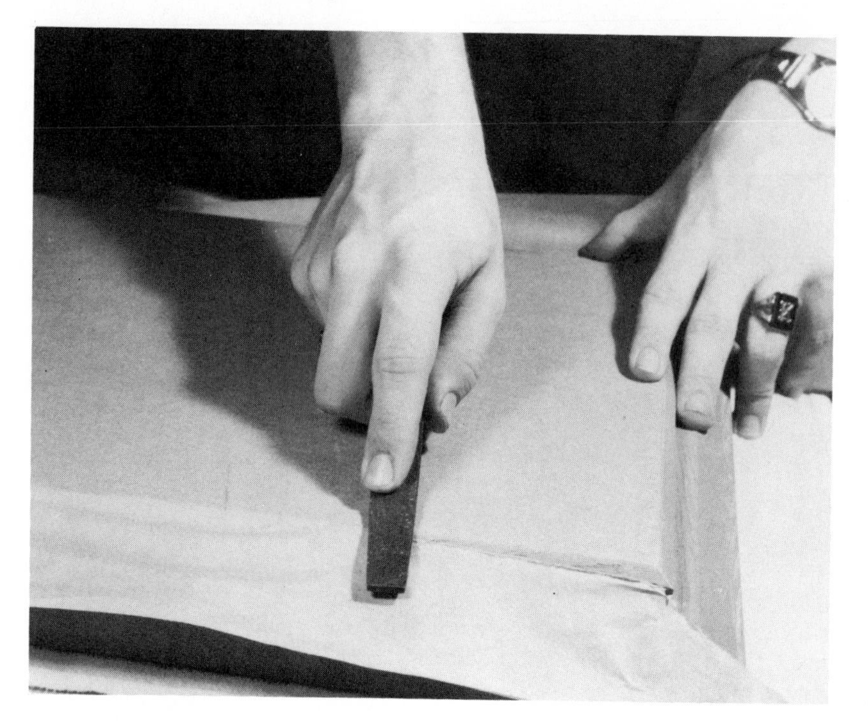

Installing Picture Frame Wire

The first step in placing the wire to hang the frame is to measure an equal distance down from the top, on both sides of the frame. Then make a hole in which to start the screw eye with an icepick or a nail.

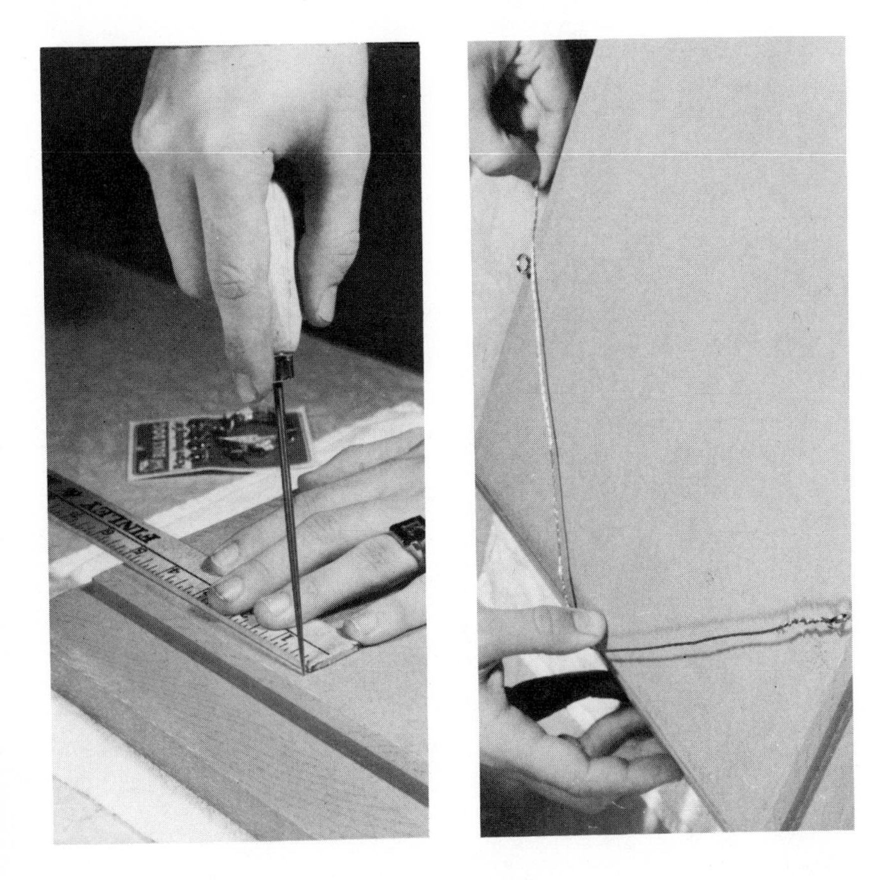

Install screw eyes and picture frame wire. Twist one end of the wire to fasten to the screw eye. Then measure the distance by pulling the wire upward to the approximate hanging position. Cut and attach the other end after measuring, making sure that the wire does not show over the top of the frame from the front.

Picture Frame Without Joints

For just a few pennies you can make a good-looking plywood photo mount, and without a single joint. They are just solid pieces of plywood with beveled edges.

Saw the frame so that the inside front face of the mount is about 1/8 inch larger all around than the print. Round off all sharp corners with sandpaper and sand the bevels smooth. You can then paint or stain it as you wish; by leaving the plies visible you automatically achieve a decorative effect. A contrasting coat of paint applied to the front will produce a two-toned finish. Wipe the bevels clean, leaving the solid color to show in the margin around the print.

To mount your picture apply a thin coat of rubber cement to the front of the "frame" and the back of the print. Let dry thoroughly. Center the print carefully as you drop it into place, since it cannot be shifted once it is in contact. Rub hard with a soft cloth. Turn a screw eye into the back for hanging, or use stick-on picture hangers.

Old frames which may be out of style can be put to a new use by adding novelty items dealing with the new subject matter to be used in the frames.

In reworking the frame to be used for a picture of a pet squirrel a variety of nuts was glued around the front edge of the frame and then sprayed gold.

The same principle was applied to the baby picture frame by gluing a pair of shoes onto the frame and spraying the frame, shoes and all. It gives the impression of a bronzed frame. The shoes used were vinyl booties from the dime store—intended as dolly footwear. This type of reworked frame may be sprayed any color to harmonize with the decor; the unique frame will focus attention on the picture in a new way, yet it is very inexpensive.

Back Mounting

The first step in making a back mounting is to cut a piece of plywood or heavy cardboard for the back board, leaving room for a margin around the picture. The board is then covered with material such as decorator's burlap, which is available in many different colors; the cloth is folded over the edges and fastened on the back with thumbtacks.

Most personal of all gifts is a portrait photograph of yourself in a "did-it-myself" frame. The best feature of this type of framing is that it is easy on the pocketbook. To create the one shown above, first paint an inexpensive frame. You probably have some on hand. Then glue on two rows of ball fringe, spray the photograph and fit into the frame with a cardboard backer and a paper dust guard. The fringe will cost about 84c for the 3½ yards required by this size frame (10 x 14″). The result is a portrait photograph the recipient can hang immediately.

One clever idea for covering an inexpensive frame is to use a fabric similar to that which the subject is wearing, as in the photograph of the child in striped pajamas: the frame is covered with a narrow striped seersucker.

First buy an inexpensive frame. This one was only $1.19 for a 10 x 12″ frame. Half a yard of seersucker costs 62 cents. You will also need six nails and a cardboard backing for the photograph.

Cut fabric to fit each side of the frame and glue each side separately, overlapping slightly and mitering the corners. Decorate with appliqué (about 75c), spray the photograph, and fit into the frame. Cut plain wrapping paper to fit the back and glue to the rim of the frame as a dust guard.

The childhood charms of this "Wee Willie Winkie" have been captured forever in a portrait photograph that will grow more valuable with the passing of each year.

It is not always necessary for all frames in a grouping to match. Just be sure—as we have emphasized previously—that the various pictures are not splattered on the wall. Brilliant irridescent orange upholstery in this panelled dining room is counterbalanced by a wall treatment including six portrait photographs in frames from the House of Heydenryk. Arrangement features interesting sofa seating for dining. Frames blend well with panelled wall; the same grouping would be too ornate on a plain wall. Notice that none of the frames match, yet by careful arrangement they blend into a group. Each picture is framed to suit the individual portrait.

The frames are all matched to unify the grouping. Simple frames are in keeping with the wall and other surroundings. A large wall clock is made a part of the group by hanging it next to it. The pictures make an interesting focal point and add charm to a pleasant breakfast nook.

On the following pages are shown four frames made by Robert Kulicke, a frame-maker who is the first choice of many museums when it comes to selecting frames for paintings and photographs.

These frames were created to make the not-so-easy art of frame construction a little easier for himself and the harried photographer. The prominent feature is that all of these frames are demountable. In other words, the pictures can be temporarily retired from demountable frames and new photographs dropped into place in minutes. It is a matter of selecting the frame for your particular needs or taste.

Many of these frames can be bought at leading art stores throughout the country, but if you can't find them, write to Kulicke, 1007 Madison Ave., New York, N. Y. 10021.

The Minute Mount frame is one that can be fitted together with four moves. It consists of four metal grooved edges which are made to fit over the borders around the picture or mount board edge. The picture is sandwiched between the back plate and a front plate of glass. The back plate has a secondary raised molding on the back side, which is invisible when the frame is hanging. This holds the frame away from the wall.

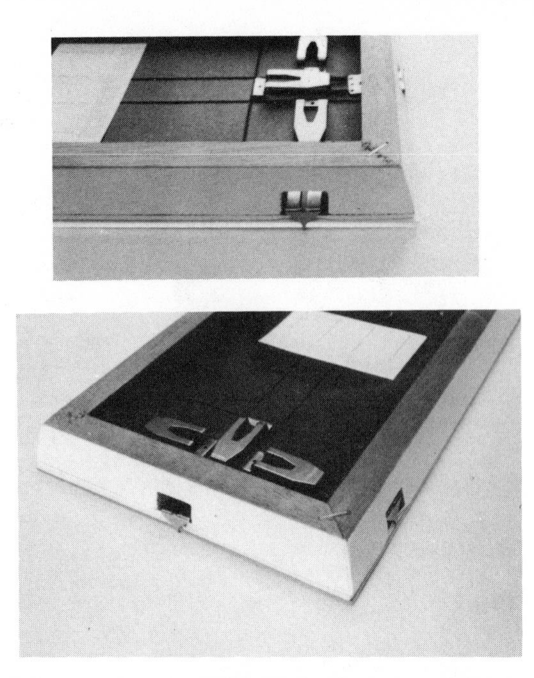

The Clip Frame is an especially easy way to mount or dismount pictures. Clamps that can be quickly flipped open from behind hold the edges of the picture on all sides. The picture is covered with a clear plastic surface. This front piece, along with the picture underneath is held tightly in place by arrow-like teeth at six points. The frame is beveled so that the picture seems to be floating on the wall. The frame is unseen from the front.

This polished aluminum frame gives a smart appearance. Pictures are fastened in place by inserting four screws, one on each side of the frame. This one is a favorite of museums.

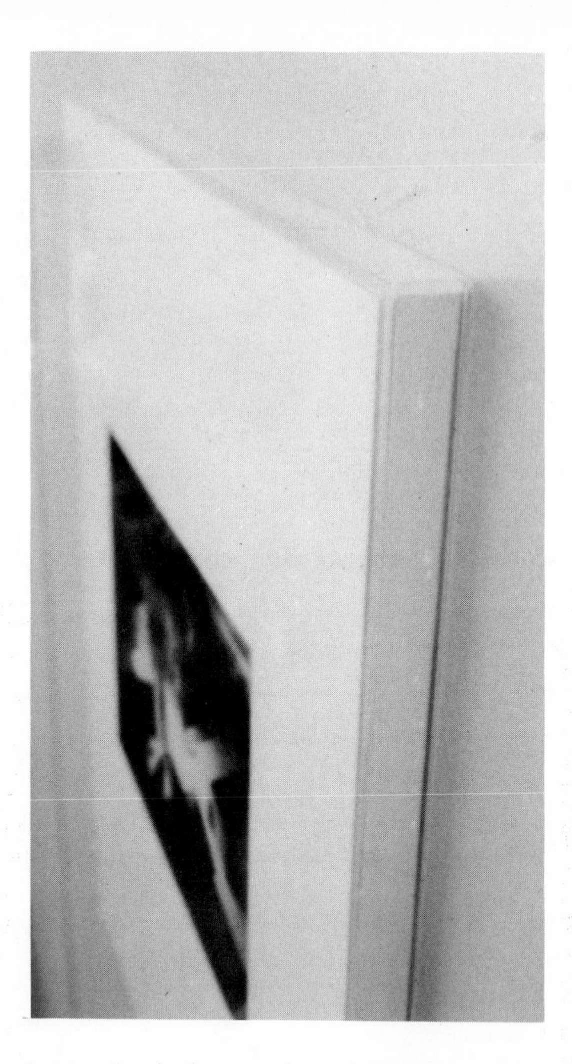

A museum type, plastic frame gives the photograph a borderless feeling, although the frame is visible. The entire frame, including the edges, is made of transparent, clean looking plastic.

ROGUES GALLERY
OF THE
ROGER RAYMONDS

CHAPTER 7

Unusual Ways To Show Off Your Pictures

Photo decorating ideas may come from anywhere. It's up to you to look for opportunities to use your own ingenuity in displaying your favorite photographs. Don't let your decorating show the results of a lazy mind. Let the following chapter be the inspiration that sparks an idea which you can use effectively in your home.

Rogues' Gallery

Instead of skeletons in the closet, this family came up with a novel way of keeping the family tree in its closet. The "tree" is made up of portraits of members of the family hung in a grouping on the inside or back of a linen closet door. Neat metal frames harmonize well with the pictures and background. Of course, this idea will not be very attractive unless the closet itself is decorated to make it attractive when the door is open. A simple sign adds to the effectiveness of the display. Such a grouping may not fit in with the decor of the room, but by hanging them in this way they are permanently framed and out of the way, yet they can be viewed by simply opening the door.

Carry Pictures to College

The idea of decorating with photographs of family and friends need not be limited only to the home. When the college student returns to the campus, pictures can go along as a reminder of the folks at home.

These pictures can decorate the coed's dressing room in an exciting way by being incorporated into a modern triptych. This triptych is a new version of an ancient altarpiece with a center panel and two flanking panels half its size that fold over. The entire unit can be stored or moved easily, since it folds flat. In this modern version of the triptych, the center panel is a mirror. Portrait photos adorn the flanking panels.

This triptych is made with a plywood back, using plain molding to frame the panels. To finish the side panels, cut a piece of cardboard to fit each frame; then select portrait photographs from the family album, and arrange three photographs on each piece of cardboard. Trim the pictures to fit and glue them in place with rubber cement. Last, attach the molding and screw two hinges on each side of the center panel and fasten them to the side panels. Be sure to space the hinges identically on each side for best results.

This idea can be used for the teenager's room at home, as well as for the young college student who wishes to have the security of family and friends when he is away from home for the first time. A variation of the triptych could be to use the center panel as a bulletin board.

Photo On Coffee Table

The glass top of a coffee table is one of the simplest ways to show off your favorite photos. It is a simple matter to slip a picture under the glass, as shown below. In this case an aerial photograph was made to fit the width of the table. If you cannot make your own pictures you can purchase aerial photographs of your home town from the Photographic Department of the U. S. Department of Agriculture in Washington, D. C. Their staff includes some of the finest aerial photographers, and their reprint prices are very inexpensive even for larger pictures suitable for murals. The United States Department of Agriculture will give prices on request; be sure to include the name of your city, county, and state.

If you do not wish to use a glass top on your coffee table, you may make a photographic top by gluing the photo to the table and then covering the entire table with a clear spray coating or lacquer. The finished product is handsome enough for the living room, but not tough enough for the outdoors.

Another idea for a table-top display of pictures is a grouping of photographs of places you have visited in your home state, arranged around a map of the state. Either of these table-top groupings will make a good conversation piece for living room or den.

Photo Candle

The candle is traditionally an item in Christmas decor. You can make it a unique part of a home year-round by making a personalized, illuminated picture holder out of the candle. It also makes a fine gift.

You'll need a cylindrical jar or glass, without a taper. The jar used in the illustrations is five inches tall and three inches in diameter. If your jar is too tall in relation to its width, the candle won't burn well.

Place a short candle inside the jar. This can be done easily by first lighting the candle and letting some wax drip down inside the jar to the bottom. Quickly blow out the candle and place it inside the jar before the wax cools. Hold in place for a few seconds until it cools, and it will be stuck firmly to the bottom. If the jar is too tall or too narrow you will have trouble getting your hand inside.

Next, choose a picture and glue it to the outside of the jar. Trim away any excess from the print, including the borders. A horizontal composition, naturally, lends itself best to this type of mounting.

Spread glue around the rim of the jar and sprinkle multicolored glitter on before the glue dries (a newspaper underneath will catch the excess).

Single-weight pictures will transmit the light very well. Since the particular picture used in the illustration is an infra-red photograph which, when illuminated, has a highly unusual quality. The fence in the picture adds to the composition since it runs all the way around the jar.

In this case, there were no edges to conceal; if you cannot make a picture fit your jar exactly you may easily add a strip of colored paper, aluminum foil, or decorative ribbon or braid.

Photographic Place Mats

You can easily make attractive, personalized place mats for your dining room table by mounting enlargements of your favorite pictures on them. Landscapes, seascapes, and snow scenes are appropriate, as are groups of small pictures of related subjects printed on a single large sheet of paper. Sports and vacation activities and family groups also make good photomontages. The important thing is that the subject matter crop to best advantage in a horizontal composition.

Prints may have borders, but usually look better without them. Since most photographic papers shrink slightly after processing, the support board should not be measured until the print is made and trimmed. The picture need not be black and white; a sepia-toned print will harmonize with dark table woods, and blue or gold-toned photographs will be very effective with the light, modern furniture. Hand-colored or natural color prints can be harmonized with color schemes of the decor.

An important step is needed for protection of the print surface against damage by spilled foods or liquids. This may be done by coating the mounted print with a clear varnish or plastic coating. Aerosol sprays make this step easy. Three coats are best. Another method would be to laminate the print with plastic.

These photographic pieces are brilliant and attractive. Your completed place mat will be both decorative and utilitarian, and will grace any table.

Photographic Book Ends

Unique book ends can be made from scraps of wood, screws and a negative taken of your subject in a sitting or leaning position. Make two enlargements of the subject, then reverse the negative and make two more. Mount two of the prints on thin wood or photo mount board, cut around the outline of the image very carefully, then mount the remaining prints on the opposite sides, taking care to align it with picture on the other side. Cut out a base and back for the bookends and glue the cutouts in place. For best results you should have at least three contact points.

Wall Mural

Are you looking for a place to head when you get fed up with the everyday business of earning a living, bucking the traffic, and meeting all the responsibilities? We all need time off once in a while! Somewhere in your own heart and mind you may treasure you own idea of a favorite resting place. You can convert your wall into a serene and beautiful outdoor scene. As life speeds on about you and you speed to meet its pace, turn when you can to lose yourself for a moment or two in the calm isolation provided by a wall mural. These wall murals are available from the Louis F. Dow Company, St. Paul, Minnesota, and are easy to hang.

Comic Photo Plaques

Despite progress there are still some walls which are tiresome to look at: these are usually ones on which the same old pictures have hung in the same spots year after year until they seem as though they grow out of the plaster. It seems only reasonable that such comparatively inexpensive items as pictures might be replaced now and then—or at any rate shifted about for the sake of variety. The following is one way of imparting new life to a tired old wall.

Those of you who read the funny papers will have observed a trick employed by a well-known cartoonist. In his cartoons of room interiors there often appear little pictures on the walls. The people in them are always engaged in some impossible antics: hanging onto the frame, jumping right out of it or frolicking with a neighboring character in another picture. The whole idea is ludicrous and adds immensely to the humor of the strip. The same idea can be used to enliven your own walls.

To make a set of comic plaques you need little more than a camera, members of the family or friends who are willing to temporarily abandon dignity, and a big slab of imagination. Use of a light-colored wall as a background will make cutting out the images easier.

The plaques shown here are 5 x 7″—a good size for most walls. Any printing paper surface will do, but if you plan to add color to the finished print, be certain to use a suitable paper. Remember to keep the individual figures in proportion to one another when enlarging, and avoid intentional exaggeration in size between figures. Such practice smacks of trick photography: eventually the novelty wears off and any real humor the idea originally possessed is lost.

When the prints are ready, mount them on heavy cardboard or plywood. Cut away the background from the figures, being careful not to slice off any essential parts (cardboard can be cut with razor blade or knife, plywood will require a jig saw). Finish off any rough edges with file and sandpaper and if necessary complete the job with a coat of paint, preferably white, around the edges.

It is much easier to mount the photos on a cardboard backing. The actual mounting in the frame will depend on the individual characteristic of the picture. In some cases you will find it best to cut out the picture completely for a plaque effect. These cutouts are given additional support by inserting strips of white cardboard at the bottom of the frame. The bottom of the cutouts are fastened to these strips of cardboard.

As shown, one of the pair of pictures is mounted full in the frame, while the matching picture playfully projects over the edges of the frame and is actually mounted on the front of it. In other cases you may want to extend only an arm, leg, or other part of the body over the edge of the frame.

Mount the cutout to the base and to the frame where it extends over the edges, and fix a tiny screw eye or picture hook to the back of the frame or blocks. And there you have a set of comic photo plaques fit to bring forth many a complimentary pat on the back and plenty of hearty laughs—if you put just the right amount of whimsical humor into the subject matter.

Certainly nothing like these photographs could be purchased anywhere, and what could be more novel and welcome than a set as a gift for your friends? The personal element alone makes such a gift almost priceless, uncommonly so when the subject matter is of a whimsical nature and the technical work carefully done. These plaques are designed primarily for the informal room, and game and rumpus rooms will be their natural habitat. But they are by no means limited to that part of the house. You could plan a set for the guest room, or the bedroom, where the subject matter might center around details of everyday home-life. Little domestic affairs always provide clever ideas for pictures. They need not always be humorous, although humor seems to provide the most fitting background and stimulus for ideas.

Photo "Paintings"

Lovely pictures that look just like oil paintings on canvas may be made from any favorite prints you have, or from calendars or magazine covers which you want to preserve.

1. Place the picture on a solid background such as a piece of plywood or sturdy cardboard. Over it stretch a good grade of cheesecloth and anchor on the back with thumb tacks.

2. Now cover the surface with clear plastic spray paint. Three coats are best and the surface must be completely dry after each application before the next coat is sprayed on.

3. You will receive many compliments on your "oil paintings" and will get much enjoyment from them, as gifts or home decorations.

Photo Lamp Shade

The lampshade illustrated demonstrates another way in which this linen material may be used in decorating. The picture on the lampshade is an actual photograph printed on photo linen which, due to its transparent character, can be illuminated from the rear. Another application can be seen in the background where the same product was used to reproduce a mural type print of an aerial scene onto a windowshade.

This new product is distributed by Major Photo Distributors, 893 McLean Avenue, Yonkers, New York, and is quite easy to use, even for the amateur. It is a strong, transparent linen material which produces photos equal in quality to that of paper photos, and without the necessity of using special chemical formulas, set-up, or handling. It is not necessary to use extra large trays, as the material becomes limp, and folds; it can even be put in a bucket to develop, fix or wash. Drying is accomplished by hanging in the air. The emulsion can stand repeated washing, drying and ironing.

Photos on Linen

The photos shown here give an idea of some of the applications of pictures being printed on linen. Faces of the dolls are actually the faces of the children holding them. Their pictures were printed on photo linen, then attached to the dolls' heads. It is a novel idea that will be fun to do, and will particularly delight your children.

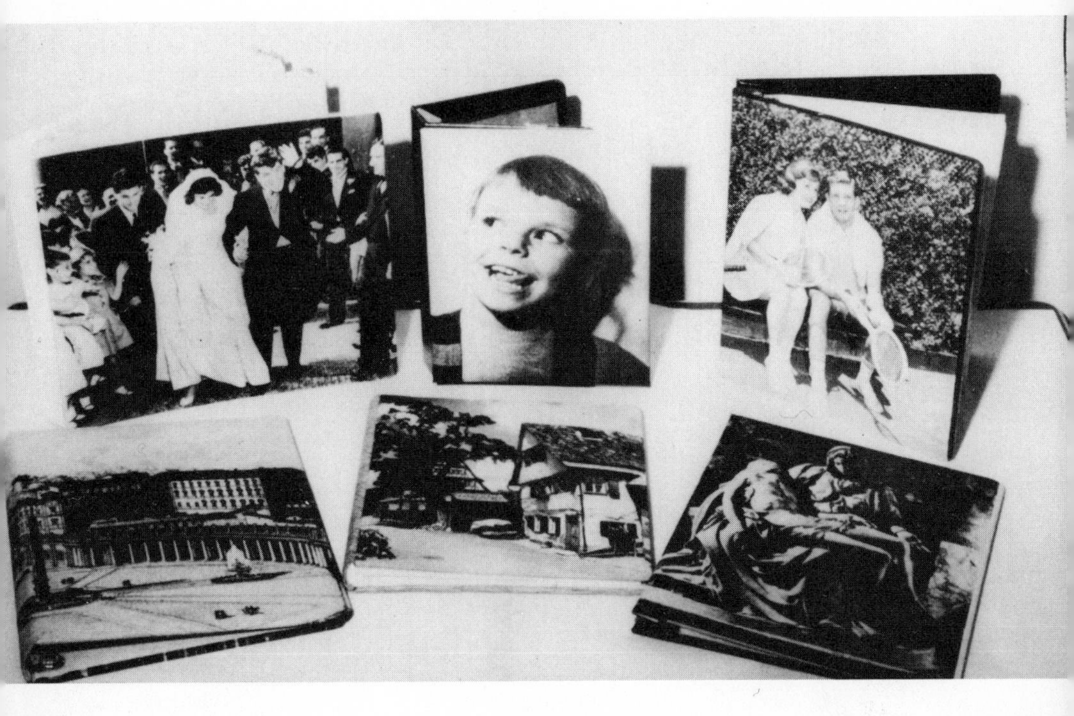

Many are discovering the virtues of photo linen. When dry-mounted on Masonite, with edges beveled, beautiful results are obtained and washability permits exhibiting without frames and glass. Don't be surprised to see your little daughter carrying her own look-alike doll around or your teenage daughter wearing pictures all over her clothes. And, when your wife redecorates, you may find a scenic mural, lampshade, or windowshade in the living room, bedroom, or den.

Photo linen can be toned in the same manner as regular photo paper, painted on, toned, colored with oils, and made fireproof. It can conveniently be rolled and thus shipped at less expense than the paper.

Shadow Boxes

For handsome, decorator-styled shadow box frames to set off your favorite photograph or floral arrangement, Reynolds Do-It-Yourself Aluminum Foil is the perfect answer. No hammers, nails, pliers are needed—a sheet of the aluminum (cloverleaf pattern), shears or scissors, and a few minutes of your time.

Corners are pinched in by hand to hold the shadow box shape. For colors other than natural aluminum finish, simply paint frame with spray or brush. (Clean aluminum first with a mixture of ½ cup vinegar and a quart of water to remove any trace of grease.) For two-tone frames, paint center section first; then use paper pattern to cover center while sides are sprayed. Pictures can be mounted with rubber cement.

Hardware Cloth

Here we show two uses of an item found at any hardware store —hardware cloth. It is actually a heavy gauge screen wire available in various width rolls. There are two types: one has ¼-inch squares, as shown in the illustration, and the other size has ½-inch squares.

In one application the hardware cloth was stretched across the frame at the back and mounted in this position. It acts as an open mat for the picture, giving the impression of floating in space. The picture is mounted with rubber cement, and the frame and wire are sprayed the same color.

The other version is used altogether for the frame, by first cutting the cloth about three inches larger than the picture all the way around. Then after a coat of paint, the corners are cut out with tin snips and the wire rolled up to form a unique frame.

Photo Heart

Builders' supply stores can yield many items which may be converted to means for displaying your pictures in a unique and original manner. On one trip to the local store I picked up an extra piece of vinyl floor tile, along with a decorative drawer pull. The square of tile has shiny specks of gold scattered over the surface and looks very expensive and different. The drawer pull has a ring attached to a heart-shaped mount. This seemed to be a good combination for mounting a child's picture. I glued the picture in the center, after first cutting it in the shape of a circle by placing a plate over the picture for a pattern. Glue holds both the picture and the heart shaped hanger in place.

Photo Scroll

The idea shown here is an inexpensive way to decorate a den or family room. The mount for the picture is a window shade purchased for one dollar. To make the scroll type mount: take the shade from the wooden roller, mount the pictures on the lower portion of the shade (rubber cement proved to be the easiest method of mounting), then make a rope for hanging the scroll. This one was plaited from yarns of various colors.

Another method of mounting pictures for display is very similar to a scroll; an inexpensive cloth is used as the background. The picture can be mounted with rubber cement, or, if the photo mount is thick enough, hung by tacks inserted from the back of the cloth.

At both the top and bottom, two strips of molding are used to complete the decoration and to stretch the material tightly. The cloth edges are held between the pieces of molding, fastened by tacking the molding together from behind. For best results, place some glue between the slats before tacking. Be sure to use tacks that will not penetrate all the way through the front of the molding.

Photo Wall Calendar

Another unusual way to display your pictures is to make a personalized photo calendar with a different photograph for each month of the year.

Mat board may be used for the mount, or you may add a bit of color to the room by using colored art paper. Photograph and calendar are mounted together, with one picture for each month. Punch a hole at the center of the top for hanging.

You can find calendars in the five-and-ten and stationery stores. The pictures can come from your picture files or use this as a way of displaying your current pictures as soon as you make them. What better way can you have for displaying your children's pictures as they grow from month to month than using informal, seasonal pictures?

Picture On A Plate

Use the trusty rubber cement to mount a photograph on a plate for hanging. Hangers are available for plates, but this decorative plate had openings around the edge suitable for inserting a ribbon which was also used to hang it.

Light Globe Frame

This inexpensive stand-up frame was made from a decorative plastic electric light globe, the kind that fits onto the bulb of a ceiling light fixture by means of a wire frame that slips over the bulb.

To use as a picture frame, remove the wire frame from the center, and glue a mounted photograph to the edges of the center section. The picture is supported by the edges only, since the center is open. Before mounting, the photo will need to be measured and trimmed to fit over the opening.

Pegboard Photo Displays

There are many different ways that pegboard or perforated hardboard may be used in decorating, serving the dual purpose of a wallboard and a backing for photographs.

Here is an excellent way to display pictures in the family den or game room. An unslightly wall can be covered successfully with the pegboard; by painting it a suitable color and hanging pictures on it, you can create a "family corner." In this case, the corner is given more prominence by hidden lighting on the ceiling along that side of the room—the display could not be lit effectively by normal room lighting alone. A strip of molding and a six-inch board on the ceiling cover the fluorescent lighting and also hide unsightly plumbing. Thus a basement is transformed into a cozy family room.

Another decorating idea using pegboard for an informal living area is to combine the perforated hardboard with a panelled wallboard. This provides for more opportunities in creating pleasing effects with furniture arrangements.

Photographs can be displayed on the upper half of the wall as desired, and changes can be made in seconds.

Another simple method of mounting and displaying several pictures together is shown on the table above. The photo mount is a 16 x 20″ pebble finish board. Pictures are mounted in a pleasing design, with several small pictures hung casually around a key picture. The simple arrangement is displayed on an easel type stand.

Along with its use as wallboard, pegboard can be used to cover water heaters, storage areas, open doorways or other unsightly areas that are often unavoidable in converted basement rooms.

To make a pegboard divider, frame a section of board with a suitable molding. The divider can be hung on the wall very easily by installing screw hooks on the edge of the divider frame and screw eyes on the wall. Three of each were sufficient in this case. To hang the divider, just fit the screw hooks over the eyes. While it can be removed easily by lifting out, it need merely be hinged outward for cleaning or easier access to appliances.

Small pieces of leftover pegboard can be used, as in this version, for hanging a few small family portraits in a wall plaque grouping. This is especially beneficial in most modern homes since the wall material commonly used (sheetrock) will not hold nails or picture hangers securely. One nail will hang this plaque grouping securely by driving it into one of the crosspieces in the wall. The design of the decorative hook is repeated on the plaque by cutting design from cardboard and pasting on board.

Pegboard can be used in these or many other ways, as desired. The result, in any case, will be a personalized wall decoration that stirs many happy memories when viewed. It'll be a conversation piece, a good pictorial history, and a completely original effort. How could anyone else in town have an arrangement like yours? It's your own family you've glorified.

Photographic Window

If you have a wall in your home that is ugly or one that has a big empty space, it can be dressed up with a combination of adhesive covering and a large photograph. By using a little ingenuity, this combination can be used to make a novel photographic window.

First, cover the wall area with the easy-to-apply adhesive in a design of your choice. Various brands of the material are available from wallpaper stores. They come in wood, brick, stone and other material surfaces.

After the wall is covered, cement the picture on top of the new covering. Then use strips of wood-textured material to make the "window" around the edge and across the picture. With a grease pencil or crayon draw lines on the material where needed to give the effect of joints, bevels, and grooves.

You will be surprised at the effect this little effort has on the appearance of the room. The use of the "window" with the small frames over the photograph gives a three-dimensional effect. You have the feeling of actually looking through a window, especially if the scene is in color. The photograph used here is one of the scenes available from the Dow Mural Co.